My First Colour Library

Prayers

Thank you for the world so sweet,
Thank you for the food we eat,
Thank you for the birds that sing,
Thank you, God, for everything.

But Andy said Teddy loved him. He grew

God bless Mummy and Daddy,
And my brothers and sisters.
God bless my friends,
And the people I see every day.

God bless this food,
And bless us all,
And keep us safe, whate'er befall.
For Jesus' sake, Amen.

God be in my head,
And in my understanding.
God be in mine eyes,
And in my looking.
God be in my mouth,
And in my speaking.
God be in my heart,
And in my thinking.
God be at mine end,
And at my departing.
Amen

Jesus, tender shepherd, hear me,
Bless Thy little lamb tonight.
Through the darkness be Thou near me,
Keep me safe till morning light.

All this day Thy hand has led me,
And I thank Thee for Thy care.
Thou has clothed me, warmed and fed me,
Listen to my evening prayer.

Let my sins be all forgiven,
Bless the friends I love so well.
Take me home at last to Heaven,
Happy there with Thee to dwell.

Mary Duncan

Dear Jesus, thank you
for making ME.

I saw some pretty
birds today,
Thank you for my
eyes.

I smelt a dark red
rose today,
Thank you for my
nose.

I laughed and sang
and talked today,
Thank you for my
voice.

I stroked a kitten's
fur today,
Thank you for my
hands.

I ran a race and
kicked a ball,
Thank you for my
legs and feet.

Dear Jesus, thank you
for making ME.

Make me, dear Lord, polite and kind
To everyone, I pray,
And may I ask you how you find
Yourself, dear Lord, today?

Yesterday, today, forever,
Jesus is the same.
All may change, but Jesus never,
Glory to His name.

Gentle Jesus, meek and mild,
Look upon a little child,
Pity my simplicity,
Suffer me to come to Thee,

Lamb of God, I look to Thee,
Thou shalt my example be.
Thou art gentle, meek, and mild,
Thou wast once a little child.
                    Amen.
          Charles Wesley

Dear Jesus, I offer you this day,
All my thoughts, my work and play.
May I succeed in pleasing you,
With every little thing I do.

All good gifts around us
Are sent from Heaven above,
So thank the Lord, oh thank the Lord,
For all His love.

Dear Jesus, teach me to be generous.
To give and not to count the cost,
To work and not to look for any reward,
Except the reward of knowing that I am doing
What you would wish me to do.

Maker of earth and sea and sky,
Great Lord—almighty King,
Who hung the starry worlds on high
With hands that shaped the sparrow's wing,
Bless the dumb creatures in our care,
And listen to their voiceless prayer.

Emily Lord

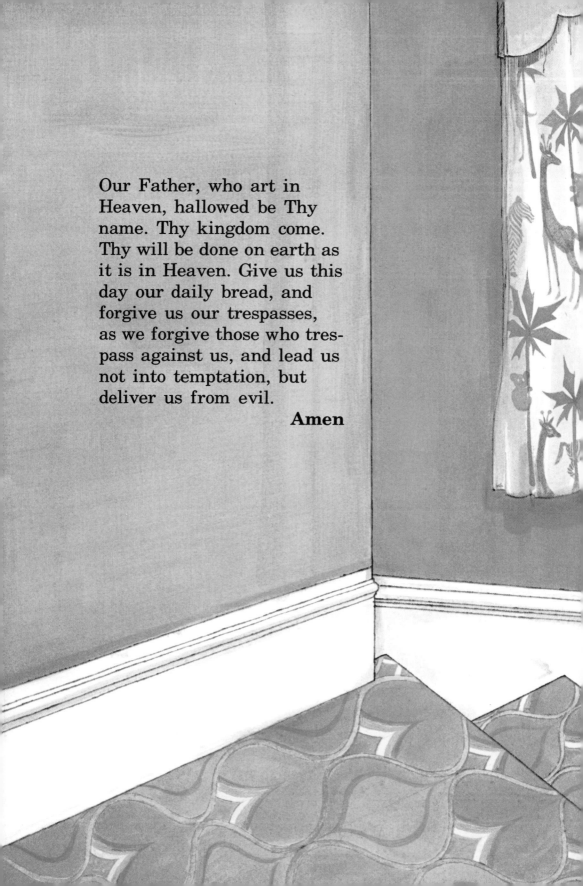

Our Father, who art in Heaven, hallowed be Thy name. Thy kingdom come. Thy will be done on earth as it is in Heaven. Give us this day our daily bread, and forgive us our trespasses, as we forgive those who trespass against us, and lead us not into temptation, but deliver us from evil.

Amen